What I Think

Healthy Living

We can stay healthy.

We can keep
our bodies healthy.

We can keep
our minds healthy, too!

Sometimes, I am happy.

Sometimes, I am sad.

Look at me.

I can play with my pet.

Playing with my pet,

helps me when I am sad.

Sometimes, I am mad.

Look at me.

I can write.

Writing helps me
when I am mad.

Sometimes, I am lonely.

Look at me.

I am with my friends.

Being with my friends

helps me when I am lonely.

13

Here are some more things I can do.

What can you do?